Bread
in the
Wilderness

KENNETH H. CARTER, JR.

Bread in the Wilderness

Spiritual Famine or Gospel Feast?

A LENTEN STUDY FOR ADULTS

ABINGDON PRESS / Nashville

BREAD IN THE WILDERNESS
SPIRITUAL FAMINE OR GOSPEL FEAST?

This book is printed on acid-free paper.

Library of Congress Cataloging-in-Publication Data

Carter, Kenneth H.
  Bread in the wilderness : spiritual famine or Gospel feast? : a Lenten study for adults / Kenneth H. Carter, Jr.
    p. cm.
  ISBN 978-0-687-65586-1 (binding: pbk., adhesive perfect binding : alk. paper) 1. Lent—Meditations. I. Title.
  BV85.C357 2010
  242'.34—dc22

                                                                              2009032681

Scripture quotations, unless otherwise noted, are from the New Revised Standard Version of the Bible, copyright 1989, Division of Christian Education of the National Council of the Churches of Christ in the United States of America. Used by permission. All rights reserved.

Scripture quotations noted *The Message* are from *THE MESSAGE.* Copyright © by Eugene H. Peterson 1993, 1994, 1995, 1996, 2000, 2001, 2002. Used by permission of NavPress Publishing Group.

Scripture quotations noted KJV are from the King James or Authorized Version of the Bible.

Quotations on pages 21-22 are from A Service of Word and Table I © 1972, 1980, 1985, 1989 The United Methodist Publishing House. Used by permission.

09 10 11 12 13 14 15 16 17 18 — 10 9 8 7 6 5 4 3 2 1
MANUFACTURED IN THE UNITED STATES OF AMERICA

To pilgrims who have walked with our family through the wilderness—you know who you are—and to Providence United Methodist Church, where the feast in the wilderness is celebrated (Exodus 5:1)

Contents

Contents

Introduction
Spiritual Famine or Gospel Feast?

As we begin this journey through the days of Lent, I invite you to meet two companions who are at the heart of the biblical witness: Elijah and Jesus. First, Elijah: to meet Elijah is to encounter a man who is in trouble. A bit of his story:

> [Elijah] went a day's journey into the wilderness, and came and sat down under a solitary broom tree. He asked that he might die: "It is enough; now, O LORD, take away my life, for I am no better than my ancestors." Then he lay down under the broom tree and fell asleep. Suddenly an angel touched him and said to him, "Get up and eat."
>
> *(1 Kings 19:4-5)*

Elijah is tired, hungry and at the point of despair. The following might be a description of the human condition in Elijah's story and, who knows, perhaps our own?

* * * *

> "Are you afraid?
> Do you want to run to the wilderness,
> to die there,
> depleted, despondent, alone?

> You can escape from the enemy,
> but you can never flee from the Presence. *(See Psalm 139.)*

> Still, you make the attempt.
> But suddenly—surprise, grace, transition—
> suddenly you feel a Touch,
> and a Voice speaks, pointing you to Providence:
> > *'Eat, it will nourish you;*
> > *drink, you'll never thirst again.'*

This is all you need, at least for now.
You're tempted to push the food and drink aside.
Too hungry to eat, too thirsty to drink,
spiritually famished, emotionally dehydrated.
You are depleted, despondent, alone,
But the Voice cannot be silenced, even in the Silence.
    'Without my Presence,
    you'll never survive the journey that is ahead.'

        You eat the bread,
        and drink from the cup.
        And you keep going.
        What else can you do?
        One step leads to the next,
        one day to the next.
        Forty days and forty nights later,
        you're alive.

    You reach the cave, and there you sleep
    in the Presence, until the Voice speaks again."

If Elijah is the model for the hungry pilgrim, Jesus is the one who meets us in our need. Jesus seemed to recognize those in the midst of famine (we think of a multitude gathering on a Galilean hillside), and he was moved to feed them. He ate with sinners and one of his most striking teachings is a parable about a great dinner, to which all kinds of folks are invited:

Then Jesus said to him, "Someone gave a great dinner and invited many. At the time for the dinner he sent his slave to say to those who had been invited, 'Come; for everything is ready now.' But they all alike began to make excuses. The first said to him, 'I have bought a piece of land, and I must go out and see it; please accept my regrets.' Another said, 'I have bought five yoke of oxen, and I am going to try them out; please accept my regrets.' Another said, 'I have just been married, and therefore I cannot come.' So the slave returned and reported this to his master. Then the owner of the house became angry and said to his slave, 'Go out at once into the streets and lanes of the town and bring in the poor, the crippled, the blind, and the lame.' And the slave said, 'Sir, what you ordered has been done, and there is still room.' Then the master said to the slave, 'Go out into the roads and lanes, and compel people to come in, so that my house may be filled. For I tell you, none of those who were invited will taste my dinner.'"

(Luke 14:16-24)

What does it mean to accept the invitation, to accept Christ? The parable of the great dinner teaches us that to accept Christ is to accept the invitations he continually gives us:

> to serve,
> to break bread,
> to love,
> to reach out,
> to receive grace,
> to experience blessing,
> to bear witness.

Many are invited, Jesus says. Few accept. And yet the good news in the parable is that the invitation continues to be extended to us.

As you spend time in these pages during the season of Lent, you are in the process of accepting an invitation. Our lives are filled with invitations. Think back over the last week of your life. When have you been invited, by someone, or some circumstance, to an experience of grace—grace that you might give—or grace that you might receive?

The invitation is clear: spiritual famine or gospel feast? We are invited, even urged, to make some kind of response. The response indicates our priorities, and my hope is that the lessons in this book will help you respond to the invitation. The parable of the great dinner concludes with a simple statement: It is, Jesus says, "my dinner" (verse 24). Receive the message of grace: "Come; for everything is ready now." So, a beginning invitation:

> Come, sinners, to the gospel feast;
> let every soul be Jesus' guest.
> Ye need not one be left behind,
> for God hath bid all humankind.
> (Charles Wesley, 1747)

"Bread That Perishes"
The Lesson of the Hungry Heart

Scripture: Read John 6.

As a kid I was fascinated with a boy who was asked to share his bread and fish with Jesus, and by extension, with a really large group of hungry people. As an adult I paid closer attention to what was actually going on that day. After Jesus had fed the five thousand, they continued to follow him. He realized what was happening: they followed merely for food, solely for the physical satisfaction that came from the loaves of bread that had been multiplied out of the little boy's basket. When he looked back to see those coming after him, Jesus said, "You are looking for me, not because you saw signs, but because you ate your fill of the loaves" (John 6:26).

Then Jesus says, "Do not work for the food that perishes, but for the food that endures for eternal life" (6:27). What does it mean to work for food that perishes? I might be in a minority (even within my own household), but few experiences are more depressing to me than a yard sale. Yesterday's glitter has faded, styles have become obsolete.

We live in a world based upon the production and consumption of goods; in my young adult years I recall cassette and eight-track tapes, Rubik's cubes and pet rocks, disco dancing and leisure suits—these seem like ancient artifacts now! Fads catch our attention and we go wild over the latest thing. If the church was once the gathering place of the masses, now we congregate at the mall; in a difficult economic climate, even that may be passing from the scene. In the back of our minds we know that what is at the mall *today* will show up in a yard sale *tomorrow*. "Do not work for the food that perishes," Jesus says.

Our hearts yearn for the next solution, our minds reach for the great insight, and our senses attend to the stimulating impulse. We are filled with fantasies and hopes, dreams and longings, all of us. As Bruce Springsteen sings, "Everybody's got a hungry heart."

What are we after in this world? What do we seek? What do we consume and what consumes us? "Do not work for the food that perishes," Jesus says. Someone has defined *sin* as "giving ultimate importance to something that is trivial, or secondary at best." Israel constructed graven images of God, bowing down to worship something less than God (Exodus 32). And in the Letter to the Romans, Paul speaks of a humanity that has exchanged the truth of God for a lie, that serves the creation rather than the Creator (chapter 1).

Jesus says, to those who were full that day and to us, "You seek me, not for a sign, but because I gave you bread." In John 3, Jesus had spoken to Nicodemus not of birth but of new birth. In John 4, Jesus had met a woman at the well and invited her to drink not only water but Living Water, which wells up to eternal life. In John 6, Jesus speaks not about bread—yes he has compassion for the hungry and he feeds them—but about the Bread of Life, the bread that comes down from heaven and gives life to the world.

New Birth. Living Water. Bread of Life. What are we after in this world? What do we seek? Do you remember the beatitude, "Blessed are those who hunger and thirst for righteousness [for justice], for they will be filled" (Matthew 5:6)? Mother Teresa of Calcutta, who lived among the outcasts and diseased of India, came to the United States on a visit. A reporter asked her, "Mother Teresa, what do you think of our affluent country?" She paused for a moment and replied, "Never have I seen so many hungry people."

"Everybody's got a hungry heart."

Listen to this parable: A traveler in the desert had lost his way. As he grew weaker and weaker in the heat of the sun, he saw, in the distance, an oasis. But then he concluded that this was all a deception, a mirage. Still, before his eyes were date palms growing in a grassy enclave, beside a bubbling spring.

Being a sophisticated person, he said to himself, "I know that this is nothing but wish projection, an illusion that my emotions crave to satisfy. I must make sure that I don't project my need into these fantasies. How cruel my mind must be to taunt me in my hour of need."

A short time later two Bedouins came to the same place and found the body of the traveler who had died from thirst and hunger. The

2

one traveler said to the other, "How strange it is. The dates are almost dripping from his mouth, and yet he starved. The water from the spring is within his reach, and yet he died of thirst. How could this have happened?"

The other answered, "He was a modern man who was afraid that he might be deluded by a wish projection. He was too sophisticated to accept reality" (David Watermulder, "What Every Pastor Ought to Know," *Princeton Theological Seminary Bulletin*, Fall, 1983).

What are we after in this world? What do we seek? What do we hunger and thirst for? What nourishes and sustains us? Do we not turn again and again to Jesus, the Bread of Life, do we not listen to his words for us, do we not reach out for his body broken for us, in the communion that we take in our hands and in the church that surrounds us? Is this not the bread that is offered to us, if we will *receive* it, if we will *recognize* it?

"You satisfy the hungry heart," we sing occasionally on communion mornings.

Benjamin Henry Sykes tells of a young boy who grew up in an affluent family. His parents made sure that he had the latest technological devices, the most up-to-date sporting equipment, the coolest games. His large room was filled to overflowing, to the extent that he could not keep it all arranged; indeed, he sometimes forgot that he actually had certain toys. At the dinner table there was always more than enough to eat, and he had honestly never lacked for anything.

One Sunday the boy sat in the pew next to his parents and heard the Gospel story about another boy with a basket filled with bread and fish, who shared with a multitude of people who were hungry. The boy sensed, in a way that he could not fully describe, that he lacked something, and now this had been given to him. He located himself on that hillside, among those multitudes, giving and receiving the gift that satisfied his hungry heart ("The Feeding of Willie," *Alive Now*, May/June, 1982).

Jesus said, "The bread of God is that which comes down from heaven and gives life to the world." And they said to him, "Sir, give us this bread always" (John 6:33-34).

The crowds followed Jesus for many reasons, and they listened to his teaching, because he had a unique authority. Someone asked Jesus for instruction in prayer. He responded, "When you pray, say: Father, hallowed be your name. . . . Give us each day our daily bread" (Luke 11:2). In the Sermon on the Mount, Jesus likens God's nature to that of a parent: "What father," he asks, "would give his daughter a stone if she asks for bread? . . . In the same way your heavenly Father never withholds good gifts from his children." (See Matthew 7:9-11.) When Jesus wanted to make visible the great gift of salvation offered to all people, near and far, he *multiplied bread* from a boy's basket and fed a multitude of people. When Jesus decided to leave behind a living reminder of the depths of God's love for a sinful world, he broke bread with his disciples, even with his betrayer, and said, "Take, eat: this is my body, which is broken for you" (1 Corinthians 11:24 KJV).

Bread is the gift of God made visible. That it is a gift may strike us as out of the ordinary, because we don't often think of bread given but bread earned, bread worked for, bread gained by daily labor, the result of toil and sweat and stress. The bread of God is different. It is like manna, falling from heaven, new every morning. We do not earn the daily bread of God; it comes to us, like a miracle. In the same way Jesus comes to us. "For us and for our salvation he came down from heaven," the Nicene Creed reminds us. "I am the living bread that came down from heaven," Jesus says (John 6:51).

When the Israelites were making their way through the wilderness, their great worry was about survival. Their basic human need was food. Their immediate question was "what are we going to eat today?" In the wilderness Israel discovered that God would supply manna each day, and they were sustained. Jesus comes to a hungry people and feeds them; they wonder, they worry about the next meal; their basic human need is food; their question is "what are we going to eat today?" and in his gift they are sustained. End of story, right? No, there is more. The sixth chapter of John begins with the feeding of the five thousand and continues with an extended teaching about the meaning of bread. "Now that you have eaten," Jesus says, "let me tell you what just happened."

"I am the living bread that came down from heaven," he tells them. The people gathered don't understand, they disagree about what it all means, but Jesus continues: "Eat this bread and you will live forever." Their concern is about what is going to happen today. Jesus is talking about eternity. We are often preoccupied with what is immediate.

4

Jesus always wants us to see a greater horizon: not just the immediate, but the ultimate.

Of course, a lot of life is the immediate: what do we need right now? "We'll just take some of the bread, thanks. We'll listen to the explanation, later." Maybe at the end of the day, or maybe when the kids have grown up, or maybe when a crisis comes. Then we will want to know what it means. Then we may want to see the big picture.

Now, we will eat the bread, we will receive the gift. But at some point we do need to know *why* we are eating the bread. Is it just to have the strength to wake up into the light of another day, so that we might eat the bread again? We are given children. We bring them into the world, we raise them, we educate them, and like baby birds, they fly away from the nest. But why are we given children? So that they might have children, and their children might have children? What is the greater horizon?

What is immediate is always there—we're hungry, give us bread—and Jesus does give us daily bread. God does provide. God's grace is sufficient. But *there is more to life than daily bread.* There is bread from heaven, bread that gives life to the world. That is the big picture, and Jesus is calling us, in John 6, to move from our own immediate need to the greater horizon: not just another day of life, but eternal life.

It is true: there is always more going on here than we realize. In John's Gospel there are layers of meaning—water and living water, birth and new birth, bread and bread of life. There are signs—water into wine, loaves and fishes, a towel and a basin. There are questions: After he washes their feet Jesus asks the disciples, "Do you know what I have done to you?" After his resurrection he asks, "Peter, do you love me?" Layers of meaning, recurring signs, unceasing questions: *there is always more going on here than we realize.*

And, of course, the same is true for us. Daily bread *is* a miracle. We all, to some extent, take the bread and eat it. I don't think too much about the farmer who planted the seeds; or those who prayed for rain in the midst of drought, their livelihoods at stake; or those who harvested, maybe migrants traveling from place to place; or those who drive the trucks to bring the bread to the store. I take a loaf off of the shelf and I throw it in the basket, and I move on to the next thing. I miss the reality that there is more going on here than I realize.

Daily bread is a miracle. And so much of life is a miracle. Two fathers are in a hospital waiting room, their wives about to give birth. In many ways they could not be more different. One was serving a small church as a pastor. The other was a drama teacher. In a subtle way the teacher had made it clear that his perspective on the world was what we might call *secular*. The two men made some small talk at different points along the way but there didn't seem much to say. They were both nervous and apprehensive. Then the children were born. After all of the excitement their paths crossed again, at the viewing window. Each looked in, and the drama teacher turned to the pastor and said, "It really is a miracle, isn't it?"

Those who gathered that day with Jesus weren't bad people. They were simply looking for a meal; living near the sea of Capernaum, which would actually seem more like a lake to us, some bread and some fish would be great. Did all of those gathered realize that it all began with just two fish and five loaves? Maybe it didn't occur to them. They eat the bread, and then Jesus begins to speak. "I am the living bread that came down from heaven. . . . Whoever eats of this bread will live forever."

Deep within, we are people with hungry hearts. We yearn for the miraculous, for bread that does not perish. As we follow Jesus, we trust that indeed he satisfies the hungry heart. He is the living bread from heaven, which gives life to the world.

Questions for Reflection and Discussion

1. Can you describe a goal that was an important pursuit for you and that, once attained, seemed unsatisfying?

2. How does modern marketing create desires and impulses that are at times destructive?

3. Close your eyes, and imagine that you are in the presence of the living Jesus. This may require a few minutes of silence. He asks, "What is your deepest hunger, your deepest desire?" Pause for a few moments. How would you respond?

4. Can you recall an important spiritual experience that is related to food or to a meal?

5. What do you think about the concept of miracles? Do miracles still occur? Why or why not?

Prayer

O God, where we have labored for the bread that perishes, forgive us.

Where we have listened to the voices of the crowds, and ignored the hungers of our hearts, have mercy on us.

Where we have recognized our need for your grace, grant us your peace. Amen.

Focus for the Week

I will learn to distinguish between what I want and what I need.

"Great Is Thy Faithfulness"
The Lesson of the Sabbath

Scripture: Read Exodus 16 and Matthew 6.

I n the wilderness, and Lent is a journey through the wilderness, people are especially open to listening to God; and in the wilderness God is especially interested in reaching out to his people. The people wonder, out loud, "How are we going to survive?" God says, "I will provide each day enough for that day, I am going to rain bread from heaven for you. Gather enough for each day. In this way I will test you, to see if you will follow my instruction" (read Exodus 16:4). Life is a test. Almost every difficult stretch we face is about faith and trust. In Exodus 16, God provides manna in the wilderness for Israel. From this experience comes one of my favorite hymns, by Thomas O. Chisholm:

> All I have needed thy hand has provided;
> great is thy faithfulness, Lord, unto me!

God is teaching Israel and us to see his faithfulness each morning, he is teaching us to live by faith "one day at a time." Do you ever have difficulty living "one day at a time"? Do you ever find yourself worrying about what may or may not happen tomorrow? In the Sermon on the Mount, Jesus instructs his disciples to pray, "Give us this day our daily bread," in the language of The Message, to "give your entire attention to what God is doing right now, and don't get worked up about what may or may not happen tomorrow" (Matthew 6:34).

When you are in the wilderness, the future can be pretty over-whelming. It helps to place your focus on what is at hand. In a crisis we see life as a series of "small steps." In the wilderness we place one foot in front of the other, we live life one day at a time, we take small steps.

When we do this, we discover that God is faithful. The manna is provided each day, enough for that day. God is teaching about his nature, which is providence: *I will provide for you. Gather enough for each day, no more, no less.* And so the people gathered. In Exodus 16:18, some gathered more and they had none left over. Others gathered less and they had enough.

This is really about moderation. What do we need to live, really? When I was a child, we distinguished between what we wanted and what we needed. God promises to give us what we need, not what we want. God does not always promise abundance, but God does promise sufficiency. And this is what grace is all about: "My grace is sufficient for thee," God said to the apostle Paul, "for my strength is made perfect in weakness" (2 Corinthians 12:9 KJV).

Manna in the wilderness is about grace, dependence on God, and providence. Live one day at a time.

But God is not finished with Israel, or us, yet. We need to learn something else. God says, "Don't gather manna on the Sabbath" (see Exodus 16:23, 26). There will be nothing to gather, nothing to harvest on the Sabbath. Life is not about continuous work and gathering. We need a time to stop, a time to rest, a time to depend on God.

For the most part, I try to take a Sabbath each week. The biblical principle is six days of work and one day of rest. Now, in the ministry this does not mean that I can finish all of my work in six days. Life goes on seven days a week, as does work. But there has to be a day a week where I do not gather manna, where I trust God to provide for me and for other people.

You may know what I am talking about. I have known businesspeople who have made the decision not to keep their businesses open seven days a week. This decision came from their own heritage and from the conviction that there should be a day of rest and a day of worship and that if we honor God in this way God will provide all that we need. By observing the Sabbath, they learned that God is faithful.

In the wilderness, Israel learned the lesson of the Sabbath. Maybe this means that we need to rest as we are making it through the wilderness, that life has a pace to it, a rhythm of work and rest, labor and leisure. You can only keep going if you stop sometimes and allow body and soul to catch up with each other. "Consider the lilies of the field,"

Jesus teaches (Matthew 6:28). Exodus 16:30 says it simply: "So the people rested on the seventh day." One scholar has commented that "it was not so much that Israel kept the Sabbath, but that the Sabbath kept Israel." On the Sabbath they were reminded that God had created the world and freed them from slavery. One of the forms of slavery they had been freed from was working seven days a week.

For a number of years I have led a retreat that was required of all first-year clergy in our annual conference. I always began the retreats by encouraging the participants to relax. There is that stage at the beginning of a retreat when you encourage those present to begin to disengage with everything they've left behind—work, families, other demands—and to enter into the retreat. You have probably experienced the same dynamic in transitioning from work to vacation. It takes some time and effort.

I then usually reflected on Matthew 6—do not worry about your life, consider the lilies of the field, will not God take care of you? Live one day at a time; seek first the kingdom of God and his righteousness and all these things will be added to you as well.

Then I read the passage from Eugene Peterson's translation, *The Message*; and I would pause, for some time, over a particular phrase within that passage: "What I'm trying to do here is to get you to relax, to not be so preoccupied with *getting*, so you can respond to God's *giving*" (verses 31, 34).

Now, I realize that most of us are not on a retreat, at this very moment. We haven't carved out two or three days, it is more like two or three hours, but the principle is the same. We're all in the process of disengaging from whatever we left behind at home this morning, something on television, a family disagreement, an errand that needs to be accomplished or a bill that needs to be paid, a phone call or e-mail that needs to be returned. So I am encouraging us to leave all of that behind, to disengage with it, and to enter into this teaching of Jesus.

Our Gospel passage falls in the middle of the Sermon on the Mount and it follows a brief teaching about money. That is not accidental. Much of our anxiety and spiritual struggle is related to money, regardless of how much or how little we have of it. This question, "Will there be enough?" must be embedded deeply within us. Maybe it is in our genetic code, perhaps we are hunter-gatherers anxious about

11

whether there will be enough food for that day. We wonder and worry: is there enough to provide for my family, enough to make that college tuition payment, enough to retire on, enough to make it to the end of life?

Jesus prompts the question: Why worry? Has anyone, by worrying, ever added an hour to her span of life, or, it could be translated, an inch to his height? The answer, logically, is no.

Then Jesus asks his disciples to participate in an experiment. "Look at the birds, free and unfettered, not tied down to a job description, careless in the care of God" (verse 26 *The Message*). Of course, birds don't have mortgages, or children in college, or businesses to sustain; but that is not the point. We are not comparing ourselves to birds. We are simply taking note that God provides for them.

"Consider the lilies of the field, . . . they neither toil nor spin" (verse 28), and yet look at their beauty! Look at the grass of the field, the most transient of the objects to which Jesus guides the disciples, grass growing for only short periods of time in a desert region, today it is here, tomorrow it is gone; and of course, there is meaning here too. The birds of the air, the lilies of the field, the grass that is alive today and tomorrow has withered, what does Jesus want us to see? That God provides for the creation, even a small and insignificant bird, even the petal of a flower, even a blade of grass; how much more will God provide for you and me?

So "do not worry about your life," Jesus says. "What I'm trying to do here is to get you to relax." Relaxing has to do with trust, and I am aware that for many trust is difficult. Many of us have had life experiences that make it difficult for us to trust. Many of us know how uncertain life is, and the more tense and anxious we become, the more difficult it is for us to trust.

We live in the most affluent and yet probably the most anxious nation in the world. These verses, along with the verses that precede it in Matthew 6, would say that there is a connection between these two realities. The men and women who settled this nation lived with a great deal of uncertainty, with tremendous vulnerability, with shorter life spans, with uncertain outcomes. Yet they were able to live in trust. The people of Haiti, with whom we serve several times a year, live in extreme poverty. They live among illness, loss, poverty, hunger, victimization. Yet they also have peace, and joy, and trust.

The spiritual question is a simple one: How can I learn to trust God? We can ask it experientially: How can I learn to relax?

As a college student I spent summers leading backpacking groups on the Appalachian Trail. A portion of the training was experiencing several kinds of climbing—rappelling, traversing, climbing the vertical face of a mountain. This training was for the purpose of developing skills, but mostly for team-building. I completed the training, but I did not enjoy it! I did it, but it did not help me bond with the others. When the training was over, I was glad! Years later I was involved in a leadership training experience where we were asked to do many of the same things. For some reason, I found it much easier to do. Perhaps I am learning to trust. Life experience has something to do with that, aging has something to do with it. Perhaps I have been asking people to trust for so long that I am beginning to believe it myself!

Trust is important. And in the scripture Jesus is talking about trust. Our spiritual development is directly related to our ability to trust. What is Jesus saying to us in the Gospel?

"Do not worry about your life." Translated positively, this is the invitation to relax. But how can we do that? We can remember that God is the creator and sustainer of all that is. As the children sing, "He's got the whole world in his hands." That's good news. I am not in control; God is in control.

Each Lent I return to a poem by T. S. Eliot, written after his conversion to Christianity as an adult. The poem is entitled "Ash Wednesday," and it concludes with these words: "Teach us to care and not to care."

The wisdom there has to do with our understanding of what is possible and appropriate for us. We are creatures, we are human beings, we are not God, we have limitations. Teach us to care—to care enough, to love enough, to be, as someone has said, a "good enough" parent. Teach us to care and not to care. "Not to care," not to become paralyzed by anxiety over matters that are beyond our control. Trusting God is participating in the life that we have been given—the work, the relationships, the mission—trusting God is not passive, it is active; but trusting is also relinquishing the outcomes, ultimately, to God. He's got the whole world in his hands.

I am aware that it is one thing to say, to someone else or to myself, "Relax, trust," and it is another to do it, or even to know how to do it.

13

I want to share another insight, which for me was helpful. It comes from the late psychiatrist and spiritual director Gerald May, who reflected on the relationship between relaxing and paying attention. He said that in American culture, we associate relaxing with drowsiness or sleep. At the end of the day we relax, and we soon find ourselves asleep in the recliner or on the couch. When we relax, we fall asleep. In the same way, in our culture we associate paying attention, alertness, with tension. The more alert we are, the more awake we are; the more tense we are, the more stressed we are. When we pay attention to things, we want to control them.

May offers this profound invitation: to pay attention without the need to control. To pay attention while remaining relaxed (*Addiction and Grace* [San Francisco: HarperSanFrancisco, 1991]). Jesus says, "What I'm trying to do here is to get you to relax, to not be so preoccupied with *getting,* so you can respond to God's *giving.* . . . Give your entire attention to what God is doing right now" (Matthew 6:31, 34 *The Message*).

"Give your entire attention to what God is doing right now," Jesus continues; "don't get worked up about what may or may not happen tomorrow." Live one day at a time. Live in the present moment. When your child is four, enjoy him or her as a four-year-old. Don't worry about what may or may not happen tomorrow. We often miss what is happening today because our minds are wandering or worrying about what is ahead. Relax. Live one day at a time.

The spiritual lesson is to trust in providence, to be still and know that we are in the presence of the One who was our help in ages past, our hope for years to come. "Teach us to care, and not to care." This is possible when we pray, when we sing, when we move toward relationships that sustain us, when we immerse ourselves in the stories of Scripture, when we look at the world and really see the beauty and the order and the design. I love the words of the hymn "His Eye Is on the Sparrow":

> I sing because I'm happy,
> I sing because I'm free.
> For his eye is on the sparrow,
> and I know he watches me.

This is the good news of our faith. It is the radical freedom of an orthodox Christian vision of who we are in relation to God. And yet it is also a way of life that Jesus is teaching us:

What I'm trying to do here is to get you to relax, to not be so preoccupied with *getting*, so you can respond to God's *giving*. People who don't know God and the way he works fuss over these things, but you know both God and how he works. Steep your life in God-reality, God-initiative, God-provisions. Don't worry about missing out. You'll find all your everyday human concerns will be met.

Give your entire attention to what God is doing right now, and don't get worked up about what may or may not happen tomorrow. God will help you deal with whatever hard things come up when the time comes. (Matthew 6:31-34 *The Message*)

Questions for Reflection and Discussion

1. What is your ordinary pattern of working and resting?
2. Take a blank sheet of paper and describe your ideal day. What would happen in that twenty-four-hour period?
3. How does our culture reinforce restlessness and anxiety? How does Scripture speak to our culture? (See Romans 12:1-2.)
4. How are the experiences of relaxation and rest related to trust and faith?
5. Alone, or in community with other Christians, sing the chorus of "Great Is Thy Faithfulness."

Prayer

O God, you are the creator and giver of life.
Take away the anxiety that resides within and among us.
Move us to trust in your goodness and mercy.
Sustain us with the bread of life,
which is your gift to us. Amen.

Focus for the Week

I will learn to trust in the daily providence of God's faithfulness.

"Come, Sinners, to the Gospel Feast"
The Lesson of Abundant Grace

Scripture: Read Luke 15:11-32.

The parable of the prodigal son has captured the imagination of people of all ages; it speaks to folks inside the church and out. It is, someone has said, Jesus' masterpiece. The prodigal has been painted by artists—most significantly by Rembrandt, the work displayed at St. Petersburg in Russia, which has been viewed by countless pilgrims. The parable has inspired music—we think of "Amazing Grace," a hymn that transcends all genres of music and speaks to people of all faith and of no faith:

> Amazing grace! How sweet the sound
> that saved a wretch like me!
> I once was lost, but now am found;
> was blind, but now I see.

This is the gospel, and for that reason, it is for all humanity.

Someone has said that there are only two themes in all of literature: first, "a stranger comes to town"; second, "a person goes on a journey." In this parable a man has two sons; the younger one leaves home. Surely this would have upset the birth order, since he took with him the inheritance and left behind the safety and security of home, not to mention the bonds of relationship. Almost immediately, if we are listening, the story becomes our story, and that is really where Scripture comes to life!

The son leaves, and, to make a long story short, independence is not all that it's cracked up to be. He goes through the money pretty quickly and soon finds himself in trouble. He finds work, to survive, not the work he had hoped for, but it is a way to stay alive. Then, in the middle of the parable, a turning point: in verse 17, he comes to himself.

17

What an amazing phrase: he comes to himself—meaning that truth cannot be imposed on us from the outside: we have to discover the truth for ourselves. Maybe you have heard the humorous comment attributed to Mark Twain, "When I was a boy of fourteen, my father was so ignorant I could hardly stand to have the old man around. But when I got to be twenty-one, I was astonished at how much the old man had learned in seven years!"

The son comes to himself. So he turns toward home. Here, the genius of the parable is that it holds together the two great themes. His homecoming will be in the form of a stranger who comes to town. The son is not the same person. And yet he is going home. He rehearses the speech, what he will say to his father: "I have sinned, I am unclean, and I am longer deserving to be called your child," a speech, by the way, he never actually gets to make—such is the mercy of God.

He returns. Now, the story could take two different paths here, starkly different outcomes; and I want to sketch them out. In the first, imagine that the wayward son is almost home, and he meets, not the father, but the older brother.

The older brother meets the younger brother. The older brother, arms crossed, is thinking to himself: *I knew you would be back, crawling home to Dad. I could have written this script. Give me one good reason why we should take you back.*

I could imagine that the younger brother keeps on going.

I ask you to imagine this scenario because this parable was given so that our imaginations might be stretched. The unclean child returns home. Do we exclude or embrace? This parable has always been one of challenge and of comfort, and I want to take it in that order. We not only hear it as individuals; we must hear it as a church. So the question becomes: Are we, as a church, the church of the older brother?

Here are some reflections on children who have lived in far countries and yet who may be on their way home, home to God, home to church.

Picture . . . a couple who have been burned by some bad experience in the church and yet have some spiritual hunger and want to take some tentative step back.

Picture . . . men and women who have had the experience of spending the last few years in Iraq or Afghanistan, living amidst a chaos and destruction they cannot fully make sense of, knowing that we cannot understand it either. They will be returning to the United States in the years to come, in droves. Will we be ready?

Picture . . . gay and lesbian adults who love Jesus, who have been shaped by the church, and yet wonder . . . does this church welcome me?

Picture . . . the single mother who gives birth to a child. Perhaps she is asking, "Would this church baptize my baby? Are we the right kind of family for this church?"

When you see the wayward child returning home, whom do you see? Sometimes a person you have never met? Sometimes your very own child? Sometimes yourself?

Because this is gospel, good news, the story as Jesus tells it takes a different path. The wayward child is returning home and meets, not the older brother, but the waiting father. While the child is returning, rehearsing the speech, the father, who must have been searching, and praying, *sees* him (verse 20). While the son is yet at a great distance, the father sees him, runs to him (how undignified!), embraces him, and kisses him.

Let all of that soak in for a moment.

We see what we are looking for.

The father *sees* and *runs* and *embraces*. Active verbs.

This is radical hospitality. In the *Five Practices of Fruitful Congregations*, Robert Schnase defines radical hospitality in this way:

> Vibrant, fruitful, growing congregations practice Radical Hospitality. Out of genuine love for Christ and for others, their laity and pastors take the initiative to invite, welcome, include, and support newcomers and help them grow in faith as they become part of the Body of Christ. . . .
>
> Christian hospitality refers to the active desire to invite, welcome, receive, and care for those who are strangers so that they find a spiritual home and discover for themselves the unending richness of life in Christ. (Nashville: Abingdon Press, 2007, page 11)

Embracing the unclean, loving those who have abandoned us, welcoming the stranger. Notice in the Scripture: the father does all of this seeing and running and embracing before the child confesses. The Apostle Paul captures this in the letter to the Romans: "God proves his love for us in that while we were yet sinners Christ died for us" (Romans 5:8).

And then there is a party, a feast, a family reunion. *My son was dead and now he is alive. My daughter was lost and now she is found.*

What a different outcome, and it has everything to do with whom the wayward child meets on the way home. Consider another scenario, one that calls for the exercise of your own imagination. If you are a younger person, that is your role; if you are an adult, that is your role. You can figure it out.

Your child grew up and then in adulthood moved to a distant city. You know enough about his or her life to know that he or she has lived the existence of the prodigal. Your child has known some despair, some difficulty, and some danger. Your child is far from home and far from the church. You are talking on the phone one evening and you hear a different tone in the voice. "Mom, Dad, there is a church near me, and this Sunday I am going to go to the service."

Now let me quickly note how we get sidetracked. What is most important is not what kind of programs the church has, what style of worship the church offers, how handsome the facilities are, whether the beautiful people are among those in attendance. These are technical adjustments that we make. This is a person who hungers for substance, for something more.

You imagine your child waking up on Sunday morning, getting dressed, and finding the way through the doors of the church. Here is the question: *If the church were your church, who is the first person you would hope your child would meet when he or she passes through the doors?*

Who is the person?

I have shared this exercise with smaller groups over my years at Providence, and one name would be mentioned more often than any other: Catherine Ussery. Those who had been blessed to experience Christian community in this congregation for more than a few years would remember Catherine. I knew about Catherine before I ever arrived: I was senior pastor of a church in another city, and a friend had lived in Charlotte, experienced a difficult divorce, found grace in this church, and had been befriended by a naturally persistent, older and mature woman with a beautiful smile: Catherine.

My friend's life was changed by radical hospitality. He never mentioned finding a program or a style of worship or a certain décor or the beautiful people in our urban village. No, on the way home, while he was still at a great distance from all that God wanted for him, someone saw him, someone ran toward him, someone embraced him.

Catherine embodied radical hospitality, and over the years she helped shape our church. Of course, radical hospitality abounds in many places here: with homeless families, with disabled adults, and I could go on. And I describe our congregation, and a particular person to encourage you to reflect on your own community, and those who make a difference.

The question becomes, for us, how does the spirit of Catherine live on among us? Who befriends the young adult going through a difficult divorce? How can we build communities of Catherines? How can we rediscover the image of God, which is love, unconditional love, as we see it in this waiting parent?

This is a well-known and beloved parable, and if you search on the Internet you can also read about and view Rembrandt's painting *The Return of the Prodigal Son.* The painting's significance lies, for many interpreters, including Henri Nouwen, in the painting of the hands of the parent: there seems to a masculine hand and a feminine hand. I am also struck by Nouwen's deeper interpretation of this parable, in that the three characters represent our development as Christians:

We spend some time wandering, exploring, tasting, experimenting, thrashing around (this is the prodigal son).

We spend some time judging, critiquing, finding fault, comparing ourselves to others (this is the older brother).

But then there is another way. After a lifetime of wandering far from home, and a lifetime of grumbling while staying at home, there is the one who stands at the window, waiting for a miracle: that the dead are alive and the lost are found (this is the father).

If you and I "get" this story, it breaks down every barrier and it unites us into one family. The symbol for this great meeting is and has always been a meal, and this is the very purpose around which many Christians gather across the planet: the worship of God, finding its fullest expression in Holy Communion.

> Pour out your Holy Spirit on us gathered here,
> and on these gifts of bread and wine. . . .

21

By your Spirit make us one with Christ,
    one with each other,
    and one in ministry to all the world,
until Christ comes in final victory
    and we feast at his heavenly banquet.
        (Service of Word and Table I,
        The United Methodist Hymnal, page 10)

The Methodist movement flourished in eighteenth-century England because of its deep and profound sense of the abundant grace of God. This was evident in the practice of John Wesley, who took the message of the good news to coal miners, who took the additional step of providing access to education for their children (the Kingswood School), and who saw the world as his parish. This sense of grace was also present in the mind and heart of his brother Charles, who "got it"—this gospel of grace—and his words of invitation are for every one of us:

Come, sinners, to the gospel feast;
let every soul be Jesus' guest.
Ye need not one be left behind,
for God hath bid all humankind.

Within this brief hymn fragment is contained a world of insight: the invitation is to sinners (Jesus told stories about this invitation; see Luke 14 and the parable of the great dinner), and the invitation to sinners is not to punishment but to a feast, a gospel feast that combines the material (food) and the spiritual (good news). In case we might have assumed incorrectly, the invitation is inclusive: "let every soul" be invited, and furthermore, we are to be the guests of none other than Jesus himself. What a connection!

No one is to be left behind. This was the motivation for the telling of three parables in Luke 15, as some complained about Jesus' practice of eating with sinners. He told stories about lost sheep, lost coins, and lost members of the family. Even if ninety-nine sheep were in the fold, the shepherd would go and find the one that was lost: "Ye need not one be left behind." For clearly God's interest is in the recovery of all that is lost. The very nature of God is abundant grace and radical hospitality.

As sinners we hear this message as good news! We also become aware that it contains both *gift* and *call*—*gift*, in that we are included, a place at this table has been set for us; and *call*, in that we are to welcome the prodigal sons and daughters, brothers and sisters whom we sometimes ignore and from whom we are at times estranged. We experience the abundant grace of God, and in response we practice radical hospitality. The soundtrack that accompanies this rhythm of giving and receiving contains the very best of our evangelical tradition—"Amazing Grace," "Come, Sinners, to the Gospel Feast," "You Satisfy the Hungry Heart"—and is the very heartbeat of who we are in relation to the One who loves us, who claims us as his own and invites us into communion.

Questions for Reflection and Discussion

1. Locate a reprint of Rembrandt's painting *The Return of the Prodigal Son*. What do you see?

2. Who, in your congregation or community, represents the spirit of the waiting father? Who embodies this "radical hospitality"?

3. Can you identify a hymn or chorus that captures the idea of God's abundant grace for you?

4. Who are the strangers in your midst? Who are the prodigal sons and daughters making the journey home?

5. You were asked to picture a diverse group of persons who might be considering the journey home. Which person would be easiest for you to welcome? Which would be most difficult?

Prayer

O God, you are the hope of all who seek you and the help of all who find you.
Create a space within our hearts for you,
and create a space within our communities for all who seek you.
In the name of Jesus, who came to seek and save the lost. Amen.

Focus for the Week

I will reflect on the challenges and joys of radical hospitality.

The School of the Soul
The Lesson of the Wilderness

Scripture: Read Exodus 16.

The Bible describes our lives in all of their glory and humanity. At times we are standing on the mountain peak. At other times we are in the valley. In the valley we see the difficult climb that is ahead of us. In the valley we are tired and discouraged. This was the experience of Elijah (see the introduction). The Bible has another name for this place we find ourselves in: *the wilderness*. The wilderness is a place of desolation, chaos, danger, testing, and scarcity. Moses spent time in the wilderness. John the Baptist spent time in the wilderness. Paul spent time in the wilderness. Jesus spent time in the wilderness. Every one of us has spent time in the wilderness, or we will.

I have been in the ordained ministry for twenty-seven years, and I am in the middle of life. I have lived through wilderness times, I have walked with people through wilderness times, and I have listened to testimonies of how men and women have survived in the wilderness. What I share with you are some lessons. Think of this chapter as a survival kit as you make it through the wilderness on the way to the Promised Land. I must also acknowledge a debt to a wonderful resource by John and Adrienne Carr entitled "The Pilgrimage Project" (Nashville: Upper Room). Their insights, in a study published as I was entering ordained ministry, helped me both understand the journey, as it was beginning, and communicate this with others.

It will be necessary from the outset of the journey to be honest: *do not deny that you are in the wilderness*. We all have tough times. It helps to take off the mask, at least with someone we trust, a friend or a neighbor. It does not help to pretend that everything is fine when this is not the truth. This is the spiritual principle of *honesty*, before God and before others. When we acknowledge that we are in the wilderness, we can begin to access the great story of Israel's journey from slavery to freedom, which took them, for a time, through the wilderness. It helps to remember that we are not always on the mountaintop. Sometimes we are in the valley. Lent is time spent in the valley, wandering through the wilderness. Moses was there. Jesus was there. Sometimes we are there. In the tradition of Alcoholics Anonymous, the first step is "we admitted we were powerless . . . that our lives had become unmanageable."

As we become honest about being in the wilderness, it is also important that we not let the wilderness overwhelm us! Once we are honest, once we have admitted that we are in the wilderness, we join the company of pilgrims before us who have walked this same path. For some this is an adjustment—all is not going according to plan. One of the best things we might give up this Lent is our need to be in control.

The wilderness is dangerous, chaotic, and unpredictable; but there is good news. God has always sustained his people in the wilderness, and God will sustain us too. In fact, God is especially close to those who are in the wilderness. In the wilderness God has our attention.

So do not let the wilderness overwhelm you. This too will pass and you will be a different person. In the wilderness we are "looking to Jesus the pioneer and perfecter of our faith, who for the sake of the joy that was set before him endured the cross, disregarding its shame, and has taken his seat at the right hand of the throne of God" (Hebrews 12:2).

Do not let the wilderness overwhelm you. Turn your eyes upon Jesus.

On the way to the promised land Israel learned to pay attention to what was happening—in this way the Scriptures were written, under God's inspiration. God's people were then able to go back to their journals/Scriptures and remember that God would provide, that they were to rest, that specific signs were important: an omer of manna in a jar, a cloud by day and a fire by night, meat in the evening and bread in the morning (Exodus 16).

Surely it helped Jesus, in his own time of testing (Matthew 4; Luke 4), to be able to look back and see this history of his people. This history also helped Christians who would come later to read these accounts of difficult times and to know that God's grace was sufficient.

We can also find help in keeping a journal. The journal might be where we have been in the past, the present difficulties and struggles, the signs of God's presence in our own experience, and our trust and confidence in the God who holds the future. The journal might include our questions and complaints (read Exodus 16:1-8). And yes, sometimes a journal can be our way of looking back and wondering how we made it through to a better place.

If you are in the wilderness, I invite you to write about it. At some time in the future—a month from now, or a year, or ten years—it will help to have this wilderness reflection as a record. You too will know that the Lord led you out of the wilderness, toward the promised land. The journal might be solely for your own benefit. Think of it as a conversation with God.

This has always been the work of God—to lead us from darkness to light, from danger to safety, from wilderness to promised land. The more we pay attention to the work of God, the better our chances of survival in the wilderness.

Pay attention to what is going on—keep a journal.

You can also receive help by participating in the Christian community. Have you ever awakened on a Sunday morning and found that you just didn't feel like going to church?

This is a common experience for those who are in the wilderness. You might be tired or confused. You might be discouraged or lost. You might be carrying a burden that weighs you down. Finding your way to church—a practice that had almost been second nature—seems like a great achievement. You can't imagine smiling at people or singing the upbeat hymns or choruses.

The lesson is this: when you are in the wilderness, it is important to participate in the Christian community. It is there that you will find reassurance. Often this comes from the more helpful and profound hymns. I am reminded of one of my favorites, John Henry Newman's "Lead, Kindly Light":

> Lead, kindly Light, amid th'encircling gloom,
> Lead thou me on!
> The night is dark, and I am far from home;
> Lead thou me on!
> Keep thou my feet; I do not ask to see
> The distant scene; one step enough for me.

When you are in the wilderness, you are in the greatest spiritual danger, and you are most in need of the body of Christ. That's where you encounter the Scriptures, the stories, the prayers, the history, the strength that is greater than your own strength.

The Christian life was never intended to be lived in isolation from other believers. John Wesley wrote, "I shall endeavor to show that Christianity is essentially a social religion, and that to turn it into a solitary religion is indeed to destroy it" (*Sermons on Several Occasions*). The writer of Hebrews gave similar advice: "Let us consider how to provoke one another to love and good deeds, not neglecting to meet together, as is the habit of some, but encouraging one another, and all the more as you see the Day approaching" (10:24-25).

If you are in the wilderness, you might be inclined to withdraw from the Christian community. It helps to remember the guidance to the early Christians. Even in the wilderness, we are called to encourage one another. In this way Christian community is a gift that sustains us in the journey through the wilderness.

We also make our way through the wilderness by living with the great passages of Scripture. In the wilderness we are sometimes so fatigued that we don't want to eat anything. We become weak, and this leads to apathy. We may not want to continue on. The prophet Ezekiel was instructed by the Lord to take the scroll (the book) and eat it (Ezekiel 3:1). In this way he would have the vision of God not only before him but within him. We are what we eat!

In the wilderness we need to live with the great passages of Scripture. Fewer passages of Scripture are better than none, but more time spent with them is essential. We need to "read them, mark them, learn them and inwardly digest them" (Book of Common Prayer). Indeed, this is what it means to meditate on the word: to allow God's word to enter into us. Literally, we "chew" on the Scriptures: "[The LORD] said to me, Mortal, eat this scroll that I give you, and fill your stomach with it. Then I ate it; and in my mouth it was as sweet as honey" (Ezekiel 3:3).

At times we know the words of Scripture, but they pass through us like artificial foods that are never digested. In the wilderness we need to live with the great passages of Scripture. What are the great passages of Scripture? You might have your own short list. If you don't, these might be a beginning: Romans 8; Psalm 23; Philippians 4.

Of course, it helps to read Scripture in the Christian community, and it also helps to keep a journal in response to your reading of Scripture.

We also learn to survive in the wilderness by *focusing on others*. If you are in a very difficult place, it might help to turn outward, toward others in need. Recently I observed several people in the waiting area of our children's hospital, all with their own concerns, and yet each was ministering to someone else. It can seem an odd thing to do, and yet it is also very natural. Those who suffer understand the importance of compassion. Those who are open to receiving help are often helpful to others.

One of the best ways to take a step out of the wilderness is to seek someone who has a need and attempt to help that person. Many afternoons when I have visited one of our homebound members and I am driving away from the visit, I often find myself thinking, *I got a lot more from that than I gave*, or *Yes—this is why I am in the ministry!*

Doing something for someone else helps give you a new perspective. We place our struggles alongside those of others, and they become a common experience, a shared grief. Henri Nouwen spoke of the "wounded healer," and certainly those who have spent time in the wilderness are the best guides for others who are there now and wonder how they are going to make it out.

As we journey through the forty days of Lent, it helps to look at the cross as God's gift to us; "He hath borne our griefs, and carried our sorrows" (Isaiah 53:4 KJV). It might help to bear the griefs of others, to carry their sorrows, to reach beyond ourselves, to lighten the load of a friend or neighbor. The paradox is that what seems a task is actually a gift; as Saint Francis prayed, "It is in giving that we receive." Try it: do something for someone else.

We also survive in the wilderness by exercising and getting out of the house. I don't have a particularly spiritual reason for this. Many people find that when life is especially difficult or stressful, it helps to get beyond their immediate environments—things have a way of closing in on us—and it helps to exercise in some way. Research scientists suggest that our brain chemistry is changed as we are in motion.

I could give a number of examples of this: folks who have experienced transition in work, who have lost family members, and who have faced a difficult decision. Of course, our spirituality is always connected to our bodies—a significant amount of Jesus' life was given to healing the body. In practice, this might be accomplished in small steps, starting slowly and simply: stretching, or a walk, or perhaps a run. Then you might set some kind of goal. In the process you discover that you are seeing the world in a different way.

God gives us the gift of life, each day. Health is a gift, and care of our bodies is a part of our stewardship. I invite you to read the last verses of Isaiah 40, and imagine that these words were written for you:

> Those who wait for the Lord shall renew their strength,
>> they shall mount up with wings like eagles,
> they shall run and not be weary,
>> they shall walk and not faint. (Isaiah 40:31)

A last insight is this: *in the wilderness we are most likely to grow.* Of course, in the moment no one wants to hear this, and in the moment it is never appropriate to say this:

> "We grow stronger through adversity."
> "God is testing us."
> "It will develop character."

But in hindsight, there is a truth here. Not that the growth merits the pain; it does not. But in the wilderness we do grow stronger. We discover strengths of which we are not aware; we are sent friends who were unknown to us; we become a part of the prayers of other people. The shallow words that we employed to make sense of life no longer hold up. The trivial pursuits that filled our schedules are not that important anymore.

C. S. Lewis said, "God whispers to us in our pleasure . . . but shouts to us in our pain" (*The Problem of Pain*). In the wilderness God has our attention. In the wilderness we are most likely to grow. Some of the Jewish teachers have looked back and pointed to the wilderness, not the monarchy, as the high point of Israel's history. In the wilderness they depended daily upon God's provisions. In the wilderness they learned to "trust and obey." The rabbis called the wilderness "the school of the soul."

In the wilderness we also learn the lesson of attempting to be faithful in the presence and in the absence of God. In the temple, God was present. In the wilderness, it is almost as if God seems absent. And yet, God journeys with his people through these days of Lent and wilderness.

So don't deny that you are in the wilderness, but don't let it overwhelm you. Keep a journal and live with the great passages of Scripture. Help someone and exercise. If you are living in the wilderness, you are in the "school of the soul"!

Questions for Reflection and Discussion

1. Can you recall a wilderness time in your life? Are you in the wilderness now? Have you talked to someone about this? Have you prayed about it?

2. Can you practice a particular spiritual discipline: read the Letter to the Hebrews and reflect on sacrifice; fast on Fridays (consult your physician first); share communion with a homebound person (an ordained person can make this possible); turn off the television (!).

3. Can you identify a friend who is walking through the wilderness of grief or loss? How might you walk alongside this person in the journey?

4. Thumb through a hymnal and write down references to the cross and sacrifice.

5. Have you ever kept a spiritual journal? Why or why not? What obstacles prevent you from keeping a journal? What might be the benefits?

Prayer

Lord Jesus, you call us to follow you,
in the journey out of darkness and into the light,
out of bondage and into freedom,
out of death and into life.
Help us draw near to the grace
that sustains us in the wilderness. Amen.

Focus for the Week

When I am tempted to give up, I will stay focused on the journey that is ahead, knowing that God is with me.

"I Was Hungry and You Gave Me Food"
The Lesson of the Poor

Scripture: Read Matthew 25:31-46.

People are always speculating, inside the faith and beyond it, about how it's all going to end. Some see a great Armageddon, a cosmic battle between good and evil, with the evil forces winning. Others see it differently; the world ends, as the poet wrote, "Not with a bang but with a whimper." Our parable of the Great Judgment (Matthew 25:31-46) speaks of end times and judgment. We affirm, in the Apostles' Creed, that Christ will come again to judge the living and the dead. Our question is, What will this end be like, and what will be the nature of this judgment?

Mark Twain is reputed to have said, "It ain't the parts of the Bible that I can't understand that bother me, it is the parts that I do understand." He must have had this parable of Jesus in mind. It contains accountability and affirmation. Jesus stands squarely in the tradition of the Old Testament prophets when he offers this word. The prophet Amos, six centuries before Christ, put it bluntly:

> Alas for you who desire the day of the LORD!
>> Why do you want the day of the LORD?
> It is darkness, not light;
>> as if someone fled from a lion,
>> and was met by a bear;
> or went into the house and rested a hand against the wall,
>> and was bitten by a snake.
>
> (*Amos 5:18-19*)

This word of Jesus, of the Great Judgment, has all of the appeal of a *snakebite*. Maybe that is why Matthew 25 is so little read by those who are preoccupied with end times and judgment. The *Left Behind* books have been read by millions in our country, many of them believers, and many outside the faith. But these books do not seem to have inspired a great mass movement toward the people we find in Jesus' account of the Great Judgment, when Jesus comes in his glory. People often ask me, Have you read *Left Behind*? I answer no. Then I think, to myself, I have read Matthew 25, and on most days that's more than I really want to know about the last judgment!

If we are honest, we do not naturally gravitate toward this passage of Scripture. This is not the Jesus who walks with us and talks with us in the garden, alone. This is the Jesus who meets us in the last, the least, and the lost. When I was in college I took part in a building team that worked on a storefront church in the Bronx. For lunch one day, we were paired with members of a small church. The man I was matched with worked on Wall Street. We had a quick sandwich, and then we took a walking tour, ending in the Bowery. We went into the Bowery Mission, known for a number of reasons, one of them being that Fanny Crosby, the composer of over 8,000 hymns, played the piano there. If you have ever heard or sung "Blessed Assurance" or "To God Be the Glory" or "Jesus Keep Me Near the Cross" or "Rescue the Perishing," you are acquainted with the gifts of Fanny Crosby. She had been blind since childhood, and yet Fanny Crosby had eyes to see the vision of Jesus in Matthew 25. I am convinced that when she wrote "Rescue the Perishing" she saw, in the eyes of her heart, those who worshiped in the Bowery, truly the last, the least, and the lost.

We do understand what Jesus is saying about the judgment, don't we? I want to ask a couple of simple questions, questions each of us will answer, I believe. The first question is, What happens at the end?

We are saved by grace, but we will be judged by our works.

Chapters 24 and 25 of Matthew are all about accountability: about leadership (servants who oversee the master's work), about staying alert (the ten bridesmaids—five wise, five foolish), and about how we use our talents (do we bury our gifts? Do we multiply them?).

The parable of the Great Judgment separates the sheep from the goats. This was within the common experience of those who listened to Jesus: sheep preferred fresh air at night, goats preferred warmth. At the judgment, Jesus says, people will be separated as sheep are separated from goats. The division will be according to our actions. Have we been doers of the word? Were our actions based on a conviction that as we did them to the people in our lives and in our world, we did them to Jesus? "As you did it to . . . the least of these, . . . you did it to me."

This parable deals with more than our moral response to the teaching of Jesus. There is also a surprise. Every parable has an element of surprise. The unlikeliest person rescues the man who was beaten on the road from Jerusalem to Jericho. In the parable of the Great Judgment, we don't really know what we have done, or whom we have done it to. When did we see you hungry? When did we see you a stranger? We can't actually be certain.

The good news or bad news of the parable is that Jesus comes to us in surprising ways and that his judgment will also take shape in just that way. I have seen this again and again in the lives of ordinary Christian people. Folks will go on a mission team, or become involved in tutoring a child in a tough situation, and it is as if something clicks. The "aha" moment occurs, and they get it. It's like a moment in a revival meeting where head and heart come together and it all makes sense. "That is you, Jesus. In that child who needs adult support . . . in that young girl in Guatemala . . . in that person in my family who needs me." It was Jesus. *When you did it unto the least of these, you did it unto me!*

It is not always true that people meet Jesus in the church, and then go out into the world to share the message of his love. Sometimes people meet Jesus and fall in love with him in the world, and they come to a church to try to figure out what has happened. If the first question is *What happens at the end?* the second question is asked within the Scripture itself: *When did we see you, Jesus?*

A member of a congregation that I served was involved in the local homeless ministry. He was recognized one year by that organization for his volunteer work. He is a quiet man who would not draw attention to himself, but it is good for ministries to tell this kind of story. He said that his motivation for helping at Samaritan Ministries was the story of his brother who lives in the Pacific Northwest, who suffers from a psychological illness, which sometimes leads him to paranoid delusions. His brother travels from one homeless shelter to another and sometimes writes home. He says that when he serves the homeless men at Samaritan, he imagines that one of them is his brother.

And, of course, one of them is his brother. When did we see you hungry, and give you food? When did we see you a stranger, and welcome you?

This parable is meant to stir our imaginations, to help us see the world in a new way, and of course, only those with eyes to see can. Even Fanny Crosby, who was blinded by the inattention of a doctor in her early childhood and had every reason in the world to become bitter and inwardly focused, was somehow able to see (!) those who came to Bowery Mission as men and women loved by God, in need of the gospel of grace.

There is another clue to understanding the parable. Can we put ourselves in the place of Jesus in this parable? If we can, which Jesus? This is, maybe, the question that we ought to ask. Jesus is judge, and Jesus is hungry, homeless, imprisoned. If we put ourselves in the place of Jesus the judge, we are making a big mistake. This goes against our grain a little, because wouldn't we all like to be the judge, to say "yes" or "no," "thumbs up" or "thumbs down," "you get the prize" or "you get the eternal punishment"!

The problem is that this parable clearly says there is one judge, and that is Jesus.

We can also find Jesus in another place in this parable. He is among us in the last, the least, and the lost. This parable is really about a relationship with Jesus. Jim Wallis of the Sojourners Community has said that we connect with the poor in two primary ways: television and statistics (*The Call to Conversion* [HarperCollins: San Francisco, 1981], p. 49). These sometimes give us a concern, which is a recognition that there is a problem. Compassion, in contrast, is a feeling of relationship.

Some of us have a concern about Jesus. We see him from a distance, we fear him maybe, or we ignore him, or we find him fascinating. What would it mean to see Jesus through the eyes of compassion? This is the bottom line, this will be our ultimate accountability. Did we know Jesus in this life? Did we recognize Jesus in this life?

The first question is, *What happens at the end?*

The second question is, *When and where do we see Jesus?*

And the third question is, *How do we connect with the last, the least, and the lost?*

These three questions are related to each other: to our final judgment, which is the bottom line; to a spiritual experience of the Jesus of the Gospels; to the tremendous human needs that are present in our world, especially among the hungry, the imprisoned, the lonely, and the homeless. It is not a passage of Scripture that is intended to heap guilt upon us. It is an invitation to enter into the kingdom of God. Mortimer Arias, the former Methodist bishop of Bolivia, has written movingly about the "subversive memory" of the evangelism of Jesus. Jesus' evangelism was about the kingdom of God; his good news was almost exclusively about the kingdom of God. Yet our evangelism, in the modern and postmodern world, almost never mentions the kingdom.

God's kingdom will hold us accountable, and yet in this kingdom the hungry will be fed. This is a sign of God's amazing grace. There is strength and power in that grace, which leads to something even more amazing. God enlists us in making this possible for others. God uses us as instruments of his own transformation of the world. In the process we become evangelists, defined by the missionary D. T. Niles as "one beggar telling another beggar where to find bread."

Do you see it? We are more like the people we are reaching out to than we realize! The Israelites were taught to welcome the stranger. Why? Because they were aliens in the land of Egypt. The early Christians were instructed to remember those who are in prison "as though you were in prison with them" (Hebrews 13:3). That is part of the repentance: the confession of our need, our dependence upon God, and our awareness that we are a part of the one body.

In his remarkable and very brief book *Life of the Beloved*, Henri Nouwen described the journey of the Christian life by using the four words of the Holy Communion: "taken, blessed, broken, given."

Ordinary bread is *taken* from the harvest of the grain, a gift of the creation. It is *blessed*, set apart for a singular purpose: to name this God who supplies our daily needs, even with manna in the wilderness; it is *broken*, a reminder of Christ's sacrificial death on the cross for our sin, and our corresponding need to repent of an error of judgment, or an act we wish we could cancel, or a word we wish we had not spoken; and it is *given* to others, as it was to those who gathered in that last supper, but also as the five thousand were fed, and as followers have shared in this meal until this day, at altar rails and in homeless shelters and over family meals.

We are taken, blessed, and broken. But there is something that completes us, and that is *giving*. The bread is taken, blessed, and broken in order that it might be given. You and I have been placed on this earth for the simple purpose of giving to others, while we are in this life's journey. The ways that we give are all around us: we give the music of our hearts; we give some space in our lives to the homeless; we share our money and our bread. In Lent, this is self-denial; but in losing our lives, Jesus said, we also find them. We give to those whom we love the most, but we also give to those whom we will never know.

We give, not out of our strength, but out of our weakness. We give, not because we are perfect, but because we are imperfect. We give, not because we are whole, but because we are broken. We give, not to secure our salvation, but because the New Testament teaches us we have first received. We reach out to others because God has first reached out to us.

Because we are weak, imperfect, broken, and hungry, we have a resonance with those who are weak, imperfect, broken, and hungry. At its best, the church of Jesus searches for them until we find them, and then we rejoice in the good news of the discovery. We realize that a part of our wholeness is the finding the one lost sheep, the one lost coin. Every loving father or mother knows this. At its best, the church of Jesus knows this. We realize that the consequence of knowing that we are blessed is to be a blessing to others.

We are blessed and broken people. The most helpful categories are not good and bad, clean and unclean, holy and pagan, rich and poor. More helpful words are *blessed* and *broken*. We are blessed and broken. And out of our blessing and our brokenness, we give. At its best, the church of Jesus never apologizes for asking his disciples to give; it never loses heart in searching for the lost; it never hesitates in speaking his name; it never outgrows the need for repentance, change, amendment of life.

So in the wilderness we meet Jesus, who is hungry, who welcomes sinners and eats with them, who breaks the bread as a sign of his own blessedness, who gives of himself, even to the point of death on a cross, so that we might feast at his table and know life in abundance.

Questions for Reflection and Discussion

1. How might Christians hold themselves accountable for their relationships to the poor?

2. Do you have a friendship with a person who is sometimes hungry?

3. How have you known blessing? Brokenness?

4. Do you struggle with the decision to judge or to be compassionate?

5. Jesus said, "Blessed are those who hunger and thirst for righteousness, for they will be filled" (Matthew 5:6). What does this verse mean in your own experience? Compare it to Luke 6:21.

Prayer

O God, help us share your bounty with others,
and where we have consumed at the expense of our neighbors,
forgive us.
For those of us who are hungry, O God, give bread.
And for those of us who have bread,
give us a hunger for justice and righteousness;
through Jesus Christ, the Bread of Life, we pray. Amen.

Focus for the Week

I will allow the poor to teach me about the grace of God.

"This Is My Body, Broken for You"
The Lesson of the Passover

Scripture: Read Exodus 12–13.

A number of impressions floating around in early twenty-first century North America describe what it means to experience salvation as a Christian—you go to a rally, you raise your hand in a meeting, you walk down the aisle of a church, you touch the television screen, you say the words of a prayer, you experience a change in feeling. None of these is bad. Any of them can be good. But a rich, full biblical understanding of salvation would be a little different. We are introduced to such a portrait of salvation in the book of Exodus, particularly in chapters 12 and 13. This extended narrative has everything to do with what salvation really means.

We begin to grasp the implications of salvation by noticing the importance of *making preparations*.

Listen to the details embedded at the beginning of Exodus 12: "The first month of the year, . . . the tenth of this month, . . . a lamb for each family, . . . divided in proportion to the number of people who eat of it . . . keep it until the fourteenth day of this month, . . . then . . . slaughter it at twilight, . . . [before] the whole assembled congregation" (12:2, 3, 4, 6). A lot of preparation, a lot of ritual is in these words.

Preparations and rituals shape us. When we travel, we usually repeat similar patterns: the same luggage, the same items thrown into the suitcase, the same mental checklist. Preparations and rituals shape our families, they sustain relationships. An older friend told me about how his family—he and his wife, their children and grandchildren—rents the same house at the same beach every summer; they do the same things, year after year, and I am sure that these rituals sustain their family life.

In our family we used to throw a party each year on the night that school began, and we gave our daughters gifts. If we ever came close to forgetting this event, or skipping it, they would have let us know!

The important thing is *relationship*, whether it is with God or with each other. But the relationship is not just a moment in time, and neither is salvation. It is a process, and the preparations shape the process.

The same is true about salvation, what your grandparents did, what your parents did. A friend shared her family's heritage in attending a camp meeting, one of the oldest in the United States, the Salem Camp Meeting near Covington, Georgia. As she talked I was drawn to the preparations and the rituals. Yes, some people made important decisions in their lives at those meetings. But a part of that was all of the planning and preparation and ritual that went into it. Perhaps some made decisions that seemed spontaneous; but someone was surely at work behind the scenes, making the preparations, taking individuals to that church camp or children's choir rehearsal or youth meeting.

If salvation is going to be experienced in the next generations, if we are going to pass along this family life, we will need to make preparations. Right? Perhaps you are thinking: a relationship with Christ should be spontaneous, do we really need the rituals, the preparations?

Think of it this way: you are about to undergo surgery. You've heard good things about the surgeon. Are the preparations of that surgeon important? Do you want the surgeon to follow a ritual, or to leave some things to chance?

When God was leaving instructions for Israel, in how to think about the very nature of their salvation, he left preparations and rituals. Your own salvation is related to the details, the preparations—being in a certain place, at a certain time, reading a certain book, asking the advice of a certain friend.

In grasping the importance of salvation, it is also essential that we reflect on offerings and sacrifices. The law required, in the Passover, that "your lamb shall be without blemish" (12:5). In other words, we are to give our best to God. In churches that make a dramatic difference in their communities, this happens: in choral music, in Sunday school classes, in small groups, in risk-taking mission and service. To give the best lamb was to part with something that was valuable. What would motivate persons to give their very best to God? Because God gives his best to us. The unblemished offering is Jesus; he is "the Lamb of God who takes away the sin of the world" (John 1:29).

Jesus is the one who was without sin and yet who took our sin upon himself. God gives his best to us. We do stumble sometimes in thinking that "if I cannot give my best, I won't bother to give, to volunteer." We do become perfectionistic. We sometimes think that the good is the enemy of the best.

I think we learn to give our best to God by beginning where we are. We start where we are, and we ask God to show us how to give our best. This is the sacrificial journey, and Exodus gives a graphic picture of what this looked like for Israel: "Take some of the blood and put it on the two doorposts and the lintel of the houses in which they eat it" (12:7).

Blood. We don't talk a lot about the blood in the mainline churches or the evangelical churches. It's unsettling, undignified, maybe even gruesome. I recall growing up in a small church whose hymns were mostly about this topic: "Are you washed in the blood of the lamb?" we would ask. Oddly, at about the time the church stopped talking about the blood, a generation rose up who loved violence, in movies, in video games, in the culture.

A generation or so ago, in an agricultural society, the blood had to do with sacrifice. People in that generation, what Tom Brokaw called "the greatest generation," knew about sacrifice. In the book of Exodus, the blood on the door was a reminder of that sacrifice. Good Friday is a reminder of that sacrifice. Paul urged the early followers of Jesus to present their bodies as a "living sacrifice" (Romans 12:1). Nothing important happens without sacrifice. There is no Christianity without sacrifice.

Where there is sacrifice, there is a sense of urgency. Eat fully dressed, the people are commanded, with "your sandals on your feet, and your staff in your hand" (Exodus 12:11). In other words, you don't have time to waste. Eat in a hurry. Now, this is not an argument for fast food! We are a fast-food nation, but we are usually urgent about the wrong things, about the unimportant things.

The revival preachers used to appeal to us, "Now is the time for salvation." They might then insist, "If you don't make a commitment now, you may die on the way home, you may never have another opportunity." We would sometimes hear that call to commitment enough times—and the dire events did not happen—that the urgency began to lose its . . . urgency.

Perhaps, though, in throwing out the method and the rhetoric we lost a part of the truth. There *is* no better time than now. God gives us this moment. We can make a decision, right now, to trust God, to follow Jesus. It *is* urgent. Life *does* depend on it. Most of us wrestle with important matters about marriage, family, work, the future. Getting into a right relationship with God is crucial if we are going to live faithfully and within God's purpose. Surely this is salvation.

Israel was taught to keep the Passover.

"I will pass over you, and no plague shall destroy you" (12:13). The angel of death will pass over you. I confess that I do not fully understand this part of the story. It has something to do with untimely deaths in accidents and friends my own age dying too early. Why pass over some, and not others? Why pass over some, and not everyone? Why did I receive this gift, of life, of salvation, and not someone else? Why does the firstborn of the female slave die? She had no part in Pharaoh's evil. Why am I healthy, while many women and children die of AIDS in Africa? What do you do with these questions? It is not my goodness, or righteousness. The Scripture helps: "They shall eat the [roasted] lamb . . . with unleavened bread and bitter herbs" (12:8). The bitter herbs reminded the Israelites of their suffering, and maybe they can be a reminder to us of human suffering on the way to salvation.

Within these verses are the critical ingredients of salvation:

A story

A meal

A community

How we are saved has everything to do with our *story* and how we connect our story to God's story. We have to look within and see the patterns and realities of our lives, and then we need to know the story that is within this book. If we can connect these two stories, we are onto something.

How our salvation can be nourished has everything to do with this *meal*. Jesus observed the Passover meal, and he was the Passover lamb. "Do this in remembrance of me," he said. "This is my body, broken for you, my blood, poured out for you." (Read Luke 22:19-22.)

How our salvation is sustained has everything to do with this *community*. We live out our salvation through Jesus Christ in his body, the church. We can't do it alone. God never intended that something as important as salvation be an individual decision.

In our culture we prize the immediate, the new, the relevant. We are addicted to change, to Web-surfing, to mobility, to the pace. So it is odd that we look at a two-thousand-year-old story, at a meal that people have been eating for two thousand years, to our ancestors who made these preparations and gave their best to God and sacrificed and urgently kept this Passover.

Sometimes, in North American Christianity at the beginning of the twenty-first century, we become distracted. Our mission gets lost, and our vision gets a little distorted. It helps to get back to the basics. The way to salvation has three ingredients: a story, a meal, a community.

"Teach them to observe everything that I have commanded you," Jesus said—a story.

"Do this in remembrance of me"—a meal.

"Love one another"—a community.

Nobody talks much about salvation anymore, at least not out loud in polite conversation. But we need to remember this story, this three-thousand-year-old story. For most, life in North America at the beginning of the twenty-first century is not the promised land. It is more like the Egypt the Israelites were trying to escape. But if we remember the basics—tell the story, eat the meal, stay close to the community—we will make it to the promised land.

This will require something of us. We will learn to trust God, and let go of Pharaoh. Roberta Flack used to sing an old spiritual, entitled "Let Pharaoh Go." We must do that. We have to leave Egypt behind, and let Pharaoh go.

Here Moses and Israel are our models. Moses remembers to carry the bones of Joseph. What does this mean? The people remember where they have been, as they carry their past into the future. They literally remember the promises made to Joseph and to his ancestors, Abraham and Isaac and Jacob.

When we are on a journey, hiking across the desert or through the mountains, we carry only what is essential; everything else is left behind; but what we carry is crucial. The bones of Joseph represent the promises of God, the history of God's presence with his people.

Now, as they are journeying, they are given a sign—a cloud by day and a fire by night (Deuteronomy 1:33). God had given his word that he would be with Moses. "I will be with you" (Exodus 3:12), an anticipation of Jesus' words in John 14:18—"I will not leave you

45

comfortless" (KJV) and in Matthew 28:20, "I am with you always." God was with us then; God is with us now; God will be with us always.

How is God in the cloud and in the fire? The cloud helped in that it put some distance between the people and their enemy. God would watch over them and protect them. Sometimes the enemy is external— a free-floating anxiety about terrorism or loss of something that is loved. Sometimes the enemy is internal: an anger, a resentment, a grudge. Sometimes the enemy is real. Sometimes the enemy is imaginary.

God is in the cloud, protecting the people, protecting us. God is also in the fire. The light goes before the people, guiding their steps, insuring that they will make it to their destination.

These were the signs: a cloud by day, a fire by night. God gives us signs even now, to help us in the journey. It is a day-to-day reality, the Christian life; but God gives us signs.

Experience can be a sign. An emotion floods over us. It can be surprising or spontaneous. *Practices and rituals* can be signs. These are like the streams through which God's grace flows. These usually take a particular shape and form. *Readings* can be signs, especially a verse of Scripture that speaks to us. *Beliefs* can be a sign. They are like the frame that puts our faith into perspective. *People* can be signs. I am convinced that God sends particular people into our lives for a reason. As Christians, we learn to read the signs.

The signs keep us on the journey through Lent, through the wilderness. These signs of God's salvation are deeply rooted in our three-thousand-year history and yet are as relevant as our simplest and most immediate needs: a story, a meal, a community.

So we practice the rituals of our faith. We gather in communities to tell the story and share in a meal. His body has been broken for us. His blood has been poured out for us.

Questions for Reflection and Discussion

1. Do we give our best to God? Do we give our best financial offering to God? Do we make preparations for participation in worship?

2. Can you think of a sacrifice that shaped your own life?

3. Can you recall a meal when family gathered to tell important stories (some might be humorous!)?

4. Recall a particular bitter or difficult experience in your relationship to God or the church. Can you write in a journal about this experience? Can you offer it to God in prayer, in the form of an unresolved matter, question, or concern?

5. Reflect on a particularly important experience of Holy Communion. When did it happen? Where?

Prayer

O God, you have been with us across time and space,
calling us into relationship, demanding our sacrifices,
forgiving our failures, fulfilling your promises. Keep before
us the riches of your grace, which are new every morning. Amen.

Focus for the Week

I will remember these stories and also watch for the signs of God's faithfulness.

Come and Have Breakfast

The Lesson of the Risen Christ among Us

Scripture: Read John 21.

The great theologian Yogi Berra said it: "The future ain't what it used to be." Something new is happening. It is, in John's words, "just after daybreak." We had thought that the gospel was concluded. Jesus had said, "It is finished" (John 19:30). But something is left unfinished. There is more. Mary had come to the tomb to take care of the body. Then Jesus appears to the disciples. They see him and, in the case of Thomas, they touch him. You believe "because you have seen me," Jesus says to Thomas. "Blessed are those who have not seen and yet . . . believe." Then John makes a summary statement:

> Jesus did many other signs in the presence of his disciples, which are not written in this book. But these are written so that you may come to believe that Jesus is the Messiah, the Son of God, and that through believing you may have life in his name.
>
> *(John 20:30-31)*

Now, surely, this is it, right? No. There is still more. John's Gospel ends with an epilogue, which corresponds to the prologue, the beautiful passage that begins with "In the beginning was the Word. . . . And the Word became flesh" (John 1:1, 14). The epilogue is the completion of the Gospel, this twenty-first chapter, and without it the Gospel is not a whole; without this passage Easter is not complete. This twenty-first chapter has been thought by some to be almost an addendum to the real climax, which is in John 20; and yet all of the earliest surviving manuscripts contain John 21. In fact, this passage is crucial to the Easter message.

Peter says to the others, "I am going fishing." Now this is not like our saying, "Let's go up to the mountains and find a stream." It is like saying, "I give up; I'm going back to doing whatever I was doing before Jesus came into my life." Remember that the disciples' Easter was much less impressive than ours: no trumpets, no handbells, no flowers, no processionals. As Peter Gomes, minister of the Harvard Church, says, "All they had to show for their Easter were those strange conversations with the Risen Lord, whom they never seemed to recognize."

As the disciples are fishing, Jesus stands on the beach, but they don't recognize him. "You don't have any fish, do you?" he asks them. I learned long ago that the best question to ask my children is the one that I already know the answer to. Jesus knows the answer. "Catch anything?" he asks. "No, not a single fish," they reply.

Earlier, in Luke 5, there is a parallel story. The disciples fish all night, but they catch nothing. This is the experience that many of us have somewhere along the way: the continuing capacity to do sustained work when the visible results are difficult to measure. Now, in John 21, the disciples have again been fishing all night. Nothing. Has anyone ever asked you, in the middle of a difficult task, "How's it going?" And you wonder, *Do you really want to know?*

"Cast your net to the other side of the boat," Jesus says. Try something different. They do, and they pull in a miraculous catch—153 fish. Jesus says, "Come and have breakfast." They eat the bread and the fish, and then they know—it is the Lord!

What a day! The disciples' mourning has been turned into dancing. The psalm has come true for them: "Weeping may linger for the night, / but joy comes with the morning" (Psalm 30:5). As they eat the meal that Jesus shares with them, they are taking his life into their own lives. In their presence the word is made flesh again. For this reason John 21 is the fulfillment of John 1; it has meaning and power for the disciples.

The meaning of Jesus' resurrection is that death has been transformed by the light of eternity. When the resurrected Jesus says to the disciples, "Come and have breakfast," he is giving them a foretaste of the banquet over which the Messiah will preside. The difference between this banquet and the Passover of Maundy Thursday is that this banquet does not have the cloud of the cross hanging over it.

It is daybreak. It is the great fish fry. It is Jesus' resurrection. It is our resurrection. It is an experience of the real presence of Jesus Christ, with us, in his resurrected body. It is the promise of more than we could imagine or dream about. The nets will barely hold it, a visual image for us of God's abundance, of God's provision, in this life and in the life to come. "I came that [you] may have life," Jesus says (10:10). "Whoever eats of this bread will live forever" (6:51). It is thrilling, and the trumpets and handbells and flowers and processionals can almost convey what it really means—but not quite.

There are layers of meaning here. "Those who eat my flesh and drink my blood abide in me, and I in them" (6:56). Now something else is going on. It is another communion with Jesus; a meal on a hillside in Galilee is likened to one in the upper room and now to a gathering around breakfast. He communes with us, he becomes a part of us, and we become a part of him.

Years ago our family lived near a college campus and we frequented one particular Mexican restaurant. When I say we frequented this restaurant, I mean we went there *often*; they would sometimes bring my iced tea in one of the giant frozen beer mugs. One friend joked that I was one of their *preferred customers*.

The owner's name was Jesús; he was from Vera Cruz and spoke some English. His children were the same ages as our children. We would talk often about our kids and what they were doing. When my wife or I would go on mission trips to Guatemala, we would bring him back some of the currency. He would tell us about his annual trips home, or ask about something that had happened at the church, or rejoice when a big Atlantic Coast Conference basketball game brought in a lot of business, or show us pictures of his daughters and describe their accomplishments.

When he opened his restaurant, there were only two Mexican restaurants in the city of Winston-Salem. Six years later there were over thirty. When we told him that we were moving to a different city, you could see his facial expression change. Jesús had become a part of our lives, and we had become a part of his.

What brought us together? The food. Who would have thought this would have ever happened? I grew up eating Hamburger Helper™ and sloppy joes and hot dogs at Little League baseball games. But the Mexican food got into our bodies, and we came to love it.

What brings us together? The food. The bread. The bread of life. A gnawing sense within us that there is more to life than this life. The remembrance that we do not live by bread alone but by every word that comes from the mouth of God. A hunger for something that the world cannot satisfy.

Jesus says, "When you eat this bread and drink from this cup, I will live in you, and you will live in me" (see John 6:54-56). He gets inside of us, and we begin to see the world through his eyes. All of a sudden we begin to discover that there is more going on than we realize, and so we begin to live with *an expectation of the miraculous*. Life, the great theme of John's Gospel ("everyone who believes in him may not perish but may have eternal life"), is not only what is happening all around us—in the immediate—but life extends into a horizon that is greater than we can see; and this is a *foretaste* of the living bread, that comes down from heaven, that gives life to the world.

A foretaste. There is more. John 21 is not only about *the resurrection of Jesus,* although it is about that. It is not only about *our resurrection*, although surely that is what it means as well. There is more.

There is, what we would call in our family, the "come to Jesus meeting." Great fishing, great meal, great conversation. Then Jesus strides up beside Peter and says, "Peter, can we talk?" Peter gulps and says, "Sure."

This is the first "come to Jesus meeting" in the Gospels. In our family, a "come to Jesus meeting" is when you've got to resolve something. You can't ignore it. You can't dance around it. You can't pretend it away. You have to deal with it.

"Peter, can we talk?" What was the "come to Jesus meeting" about for Peter? Most scholars believe this is all about the reinstatement of Peter as an apostle, about his forgiveness, in the aftermath of his denial.

Sometimes a "come to Jesus meeting" is about *restoration* and *forgiveness*. This could not have been easy for Peter. It is never easy for us. Sometimes it might be easier to run away, to hide, to give up, to go fishing, or to go back to wherever we were before the relationship began.

"I've got a question for you—Peter, do you love me?" Peter says, "Lord, yes." Jesus asks a second time, "Peter, do you love me?" Peter responds, "Lord, yes." Jesus asks a third time, "Peter, do you love me?" Peter answers, "Lord, yes."

Three times the question is asked. Three denials. Three days in the tomb. Three appearances. Three questions. As if Peter might have missed the point.

In the midst of the questions a subtle shift has taken place: from the new creation of resurrection to a new commission, the resurrection of love; from Easter as a day to Easter as a way of life; from "I have fed you" to "you will feed others." Each time, after Peter's response, Jesus says, simply, "Feed my lambs; tend my sheep; feed my sheep." There are echoes here of John 13:34: "I give you a new commandment, that you love one another. Just as I have loved you." The one who says "I am the good shepherd" in John 10 now sends his followers into the world to feed his sheep.

The resurrection of love happens when the church of the good shepherd hears again the words of the Good Shepherd: "Feed my lambs; tend my sheep; feed my sheep." The fullness of Easter happens only when we have had the "come to Jesus meeting." Peter had it. Three times Peter had denied Jesus. Three times Peter affirms his love for Jesus. If you and I are going to encounter the risen Lord, we will have our own "come to Jesus meeting."

In the season of Easter, we encounter the risen Lord, calling to us; for this One who loves us "loved the world so much that he gave his only Son to be our Savior, that whoever believes in him would not perish, but have eternal life" (see John 3:16).

In any authentic encounter with Jesus, we hear this question: "Do you love me?" Then we hear the commandment: Feed my lambs; tend my sheep; feed my sheep. I am the Lord of life, and I love the world and I am calling you into the world that I love, to do and be for others what I have been and done for you.

In the Gospel, Jesus feeds us. "Come and have breakfast." It is daybreak. We receive, and we are grateful. And yet—there is more. In the Gospel, Jesus looks into our eyes and asks what must be the most difficult question we can ever ask or answer, the question that we cannot avoid, if we are to live into our God-given natures, the question we cannot avoid if we are to build the beloved community, the question we cannot avoid if we are to sustain a relationship.

Do you love me?

We receive, but we also give. We are fed, but we also feed others.

A good friend sat in a beautiful sanctuary, and his eyes were drawn to an exquisite piece of stained glass. Underneath were the words from Revelation: "Behold, I stand at the door, and knock" (3:20 KJV). In the picture Christ is standing at the door, knocking, and waiting for someone to open the door and to invite him in.

Resurrection is astonishing. Eternal life is wonderful. But there is more. Another interpretation seemed possible to my friend. What if Jesus stands at the door, and knocks, and says, "Come out; I am not in there, I'm out here. Follow me, be my witnesses, feed my sheep."

In a world that God loves and resurrects, it is just after daybreak. We are the Easter people. We are the people of hope. If there is any hope in this world, it is based upon the love of Jesus, the love that he has for us, the love that we have for him, and therefore the love that we have for others. Perhaps there is not enough love in our lives, not enough love in our world, perhaps we are not catching any fish, perhaps we have just about concluded that *the future ain't what it used to be*—and then *there is more.*

There is a discovery, a question, an invitation.

The *discovery*: The "come to Jesus meeting" happens not necessarily within these walls, but in the world, wherever the hungry, the hopeless, and the lost gather.

The *question*: Do you love me?

The *invitation*: Feed my sheep. Follow me.

There is always more going on than we realize. I sometimes catch the *Actor's Studio* interviews on television, conducted by James Lipton. An actor will talk about his or her craft, and the creative processes in the profession; sometimes the discussion is sort of self-absorbed, even pompous in a way, but sometimes it's good. James Lipton asks a series of questions at the end of each program, the same questions for every actor whether it is Tom Hanks or Sally Field or Harrison Ford. One of the questions I find most interesting is this one: *When you get to heaven, what are the first words you hope to hear?* And one actor (I can't recall who) said: *Your table is ready, in the back of the restaurant, and all of your friends are waiting for you!*

To experience Easter is to experience the miraculous. It is to hear again the word of the Lord: "I am the living bread that came down from heaven," that gives life to the world. "Whoever eats of this bread will live forever" (John 6:51).

Questions for Discussion and Reflection

1. Have you ever devoted a great deal of effort to a relationship or a project and wondered about the outcome?

2. Who needs to be restored to your community? To your congregation? To your family?

3. How might Easter lead you to share your faith with someone outside the church?

4. Do you ever have the sense that most of what you have been put on earth to do has already taken place? Might there be more ahead for you? What does Easter have to do with these questions?

5. When you get to heaven, what are the first words you hope to hear?

Prayer

O God, restore all that is estranged, heal all that is broken. Surprise us again, raise us into a new life, and send us into the world with the good news of Jesus Christ. Amen.

Focus for the Week

I will share the good news of Jesus Christ with a friend over a meal, and trust the outcome to God's grace.

Epilogue

You Cannot Do It Alone
The Lesson of Life after Lent and Easter

Scripture: Read Exodus 18 and Acts 2.

The people have left Egypt. They have lived through the plagues. They have come to the river and passed through it. They've wandered in the wilderness. Their leader, Moses, has been with them, and God has been with Moses. A guiding hand has been upon them all, and they've made great progress. It is a story about endurance, about hanging in there and keeping our eyes on the prize. But there is a problem. Jethro, Moses' father-in-law, comes to visit, bringing his daughter, Moses' wife, and her children with Moses. Jethro has the kind of outside perspective of a wise consultant. He immediately pinpoints the issue. He notices that Moses is overwhelmed:

> What you are doing is not good. You will surely wear yourself out. . . .
> The task is too heavy. . . . You cannot do it alone.
> *(Exodus 18:17-18.)*

"Moses," his father-in-law says, "this is not a sustainable way to live. You can't keep this up!" Perhaps you have heard the wisdom of Jethro coming through the voice of a spouse or a co-worker or a friend: *What you are doing is not good. You will surely wear yourself out.*

Of course our intentions are good, right? We are trying to save the world. Moses is trying to lead his people to freedom. There is a lot at stake. But it helps to remember that most of what is at stake is beyond us and our powers. We sometimes operate under the delusion that it is all about us. I think of the image of a funnel. We sometimes think we are the funnel through which everything must flow. But hear again the words of Jethro: "You cannot do it alone."

Many North American Christians have been given resources and opportunities in this life, in part because of where we were born in this world, in part because of our efforts, in part because of God's grace. We bear important responsibilities in our workplaces and communities, churches and homes. We want to do what is right, because we are conscientious and know that there is a lot at stake, whether we are thinking about the livelihoods of hundreds of people or the future direction of a city or the environment or the life of a child.

Moses had been there, working all day long, from morning until evening. Perhaps you've had one of those days? It starts early, ends late, thus the origin of what we call "burning the candle at both ends." But there is a problem: It is not working. It is not a sustainable way to live. Sooner or later we experience, in the words of Harvard Business School professor Ronald Heifitz, "the cost of doing it alone" (*Leadership without Easy Answers* [Cambridge: Belknap Press of Harvard University Press, 1994]). If, at the conclusion of this Lenten study, you want to give up something, it might be the idea, the assumption that "I have to do it alone." Ronald Heifitz elaborates: "The myth of leadership is the myth of the lone warrior: the solitary individual whose heroism and brilliance enables him to lead the way. This notion reinforces the isolation."

Why would we want to do it alone? In part because we would like to be in control. But when we say, "Jesus is Lord," we give up on the idea that we are in control. This comes to us as bad news—we really would like to be in control—and good news—deep down, we know that there is so much that is beyond our control.

Jesus comes to us and says, "Take my yoke upon you, and learn from me. . . . For my yoke is easy, and my burden is light" (Matthew 11:29-30).

Do you know what a messiah complex is? It is the belief that we are here to save the world. Christians, of all people, should know that the messiah complex is a form of heresy. We believe that the Messiah has already come!

The messiah complex is not about wanting to improve or repair the world, or make it a better place. We all want to do that. A messiah complex is all about the idea that "I have been personally sent into the world to redeem the world, to save the world, that it all depends on me." We are bound to fail at this.

Moses' father-in-law was seeking to keep Moses from succumbing to the messiah complex. Miraculously, Moses listened, and there were three wonderful outcomes. First, Moses finds a way to stay in the journey. He is able to avoid the fatigue and exhaustion, and the expectations others have of him. Second, the people benefit: their needs are met, their voices are heard. Third, other gifted people are called forth. It is not just about one person, one leader. It is about the gifts and commitments and callings of many leaders and servants.

The Israelites were able to reach the promised land, in part, because they remembered the encounter between Moses and his father-in-law, and the lesson. Perhaps there is a lesson for you and me, self-sufficient North Americans, people on the move, writing out our goals and working toward them, making the world a better place. Perhaps there is a still, small voice speaking to us too.

> What you are doing is not good. You will surely wear yourself out. . . .
> The task is too heavy. . . . You cannot do it alone.
> *(Exodus 18:17-18)*

And perhaps this was in the historical memory of the disciples, who, after the Resurrection, were told to gather together in prayer, in the upper room, who came together from every nation on the Day of Pentecost to receive the Holy Spirit, who embodied the teaching of Scripture that they could not do it alone:

> All who believed were together and had all things in common; they would sell their possessions and goods and distribute the proceeds to all, as any had need. Day by day, as they spent much time together in the temple, they broke bread at home and ate their food with glad and generous hearts, praising God and having the goodwill of all the people. And day by day the Lord added to their number those who were being saved. (Acts 2:44-47)

The lessons of survival in the wilderness and life on this side of the Resurrection are that God sustains us with companions (literally, God sustains us with "bread"!), and God invites us to share our gifts and our bread with others.

We were never meant to go this alone. God is with us!

59

Closing Prayer

God, we need your help.
Where our lives have become unmanageable, give us wisdom.
When we cannot do it alone, give us community.
Feast with us at your table, and satisfy our hungry hearts.
Sustain us, and all your people, with abundant grace.

Through the One who is the bread that comes down from heaven and gives life to the world, Jesus Christ. Amen.